CONTENTS

INTRODUCTION

ART OF THE WESTERN WORLD DEVELOPED ALONG WITH THE GREAT CIVILISATIONS THAT GREW OUT OF THE MIDDLE EAST AND AFRICA. The earliest paintings were made on cave walls and ceilings by humans during the Paleolithic period, some 40,000 years ago. The earliest figurative paintings in Europe date back to 30,000 to 32,000 years ago. Animals were painted by the people who knew them and hunted them. They show the power and grace of the beasts, although human forms are painted as stick figures.

Small statues, called Venus figurines, were discovered at Willendorf in Austria. They are the earliest sculptures of the female form, carved about 25000 BCE. One of the earliest carvings of the human face is the 'Venus of Brassempouy', an ivory figurine found in a cave in the village of Brassempouy in France.

Once people became settled in communities, planting crops and raising animals, they had more time to decorate and create. Mesopotamia in the Middle East, known as the cradle of civilisation, brought important developments in culture such as writing, mathematics, astronomy and planting the first cereal crops. People here created beautiful pieces of art from 4000 BCE that rivalled the art of the ancient Egyptians.

Only 3.7 centimetres (1.5 inches) high, the 'Venus of Brassempouy' head was carved about 25000 BCE from the ivory tusks of a woolly mammoth.

This Mesopotamian 'Master of Animals' image (an image in ancient art showing a human in the middle and grasping two animals) was painted on a panel of the soundboard of a harp found in Ur, a city in ancient Mesopotamia.

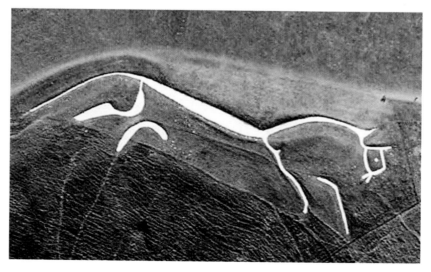

Prehistoric people of Bronze Age Britain (2500–800 BCE) constructed large works of art from chalk hill sculptures to megaliths. The Uffington White Horse (right) is a prehistoric hill figure, 110 metres (360 feet) long. It was created 1000–800 BCE.

A BRIEF ILLUSTRATED
HISTORY of
ART

Published by Raintree, an imprint of Capstone Global Library Limited, 2017.
Raintree is an imprint of Capstone Global Library Limited, a company incorporated in England and Wales
having its registered office at 264 Banbury Road, Oxford, OX2 7DY –
Registered company number: 6695582
www.raintree.co.uk
myorders@raintree.co.uk

Designed and illustrated by David West
Text by David West
Editor Brenda Haugen
Produced by
David West Children's Books, 6 Princeton Court, 55 Felsham Road, London SW15 1AZ
Printed and bound in Malaysia

ISBN: 978-1-4747-2707-5 (hardcover)
ISBN: 978-1-4747-2713-6 (paperback)
20 19 18 17 16
10 9 8 7 6 5 4 3 2 1

British Library Cataloguing in Publication Data
A full catalogue record for this book is available from the British Library.

Photographic credits:
7tl, Giovanni Dall'Orto; 22tr, © ADAGP, Paris and DACS, London 2016; 24m, The Persistence of Memory, 1931 (oil on canvas), Dali, Salvador
(1904-89) / Museum of Modern Art, New York, USA / Bridgeman Images © Salvador Dali, Fundació Gala-Salvador Dalí, DACS 2016; 24b,
Harlequin's Carnival, 1924-25 (oil on canvas), Miró, Joan (1893-1983) / Albright Knox Art Gallery, Buffalo, New York, USA / Bridgeman Images
© Successió Miró / ADAGP, Paris and DACS London 2016; 25tl, Tate, London 2015 © ADAGP, Paris and DACS, London 2016; 24-25c, ©
Philippe Halsman/Magnum Photos, Image Rights of Salvador Dalí reserved. Fundació Gala-Salvador Dalí, Figueres, 2016; 25tr, The Son of Man,
1964 (oil on canvas), Magritte, Rene (1898-1967) / Private Collection / Photo © Christie's Images / Bridgeman Images © ADAGP, Paris and
DACS, London 2016; 25bl, Self-Portrait with Thorn Necklace and Hummingbird, 1940 (oil on canvas), Kahlo, Frida (1907-54) / Harry Ransom
Center, University of Texas at Austin, Austin, USA / © Leemage / Bridgeman Images, © Banco de México Diego Rivera Frida Kahlo Museums
Trust, Mexico, D.F. / DACS 2016; 25br, © 1998 Kate Rothko Prizel & Christopher Rothko ARS, NY and DACS, London; 26tl, I was a Rich
Man's Plaything, from the 'Bunk' series, c.1950 (colour litho), Paolozzi, Eduardo Luigi (1924-2005) / Laing Art Gallery, Newcastle-upon-Tyne,
UK / Bridgeman Images, © Trustees of the Paolozzi Foundation, Licensed by DACS 2016; 26-27m, © Tate, London 2015, © Estate of Roy
Lichtenstein/DACS 2016; 26bl, Three Flags, 1958 (encaustic on canvas), Johns, Jasper (b.1930) / Whitney Museum of American Art, New York,
USA / Bridgeman Images, © Jasper Johns / VAGA, New York / DACS, London 2016; 27tr, Warhol Diptych, 1973 (silkscreen inks, synthetic
polymer & acrylic on canvas), Sturtevant, Elaine (1924-2014) / Private Collection / Photo © Christie's Images / Bridgeman Images, © 2016 The
Andy Warhol Foundation for the Visual Arts, Inc. / Artists Rights Society (ARS), New York and DACS, London; 27mr, © Tate, London 2015;
27br, © Bridget Riley 2016. All rights reserved, courtesy Karsten Schubert, London; 28tl, Fifty Days at Iliam: The Fire that Consumes All before
It, 1978 (oil, oil crayon & graphite on canvas), Twombly, Cy (1929-2011) / Philadelphia Museum of Art, Pennsylvania, PA, USA / Gift (exchange)
of Samuel S White 3rd & Vera White, 1989 / Bridgeman Images; 28m, © Rachel Whiteread; Courtesy of the artist, Luhring Augustine, New York,
Lorcan O'Neill, Rome, and Gagosian Gallery; 28b, Spiral Jetty from atop Rozel Point, in mid-April 2005, Soren.harward at en.wikipedia; 29tr, ©
Damien Hirst and Science Ltd. All rights reserved, DACS 2016. Photo: Prudence Cuming Associates Ltd; 29ml, © The Keith Haring Foundation;
29mr, © Tate, London 2015; 29br, © Billy Childish. All Rights Reserved, DACS 2016.

More than 30,000 years ago, prehistoric humans produced paintings on walls that show style and grace. They would not be out of place in a modern gallery today.

THE ANCIENT WORLD
EGYPTIAN ART

THE CIVILISATION OF ANCIENT EGYPT PRODUCED ART THAT INCLUDED PAINTINGS, SCULPTURES IN WOOD, STONE AND CERAMICS, DRAWINGS ON PAPYRUS AND JEWELLERY. STYLES CHANGED LITTLE DURING 3,000 YEARS (3000 BCE TO 30 AD) WITH THE FIGURES' DISTINCTIVE SIDE-VIEW WALKING STANCE ON WALL RELIEFS AND PAINTINGS.

Tutankhamun's burial mask, 1324 BCE

Tombs and mummies

Much of the surviving art comes from tombs and monuments. It gives a detailed view into the life and beliefs of ancient Egyptians. Scenes such as farming on the banks of the river Nile are portrayed in detail. Ploughing and sowing to harvesting crops are shown alongside hieroglyphs (sacred words) that were used to add extra information. Artists depicted their subjects according to a set of rules. Figures were shown seated or standing from a side view. Less important figures were drawn smaller. Painters had little status and worked in teams with some drawing the scene while others painted colours.

Egyptians believed in life after death and were buried with things they would need in the afterlife. Tombs held treasures of beautiful furniture, jewellery and gold burial masks decorated with gems.

During the Roman period (30 BCE–120 AD), realistic portraits, called Fayum mummy portraits, were painted on wooden boards that were attached to mummies.

A portion of a wall painting from the tomb of the scribe Nebamun (left) shows him hunting birds in the marshes in 1350 BCE.

'Bust of Nefertiti' by Thutmose, 1345 BCE

The Great Temple at Abu Simbel was completed during the reign of Ramesses II, 1265 BCE.

Sculptures

The ancient Egyptians are famous for their huge sculptures. Massive statues were built to represent gods and pharaohs and their queens, inside and outside temples. The four giant statues outside the main temple at Abu Simbel show Ramesses II (1279–1213 BCE). Statues and carved scenes along the walls of temples were often painted. Small models of the slaves, animals, buildings and objects, such as boats necessary for the dead to continue in the afterlife, have been found in tombs. Official court sculptors, such as Thutmose, produced special master sculptures, such as the 'Bust of Nefertiti', for others to copy.

THE ANCIENT WORLD
GREEK ART

T HE ART OF ANCIENT GREECE IS USUALLY DIVIDED INTO FOUR PERIODS: GEOMETRIC (FROM 1000 BCE), ARCHAIC (FROM 700 BCE), CLASSICAL (FROM 500 BCE) AND HELLENISTIC (FROM 336 TO 31 BCE). GEOMETRIC ART, CHARACTERISED BY GEOMETRIC PATTERNS ON VASES, WAS AT ITS HEIGHT TOWARD THE END OF THE GREEK DARK AGES AROUND 900 TO 800 BCE.

Sculptures and reliefs

The development of Greek art was amazing by ancient standards. It is best seen in sculpture because no paintings, apart from pottery decoration, survive. The development of the sculpted human body is at its centre. Life-sized sculptures of the Archaic period were not realistic. They were modelled in a style popular at the time and inspired by the huge stone sculptures of Egypt.

This painted, reconstructed Greek statue from the Archaic period, of a young woman, is known as a kore. Greek statues and temples were often painted, as on the frieze of the Parthenon in Greece.

The Classical period saw a revolution in statuary. Poses became more natural, and the skills of the sculptors increased. Sculpture and statues were put to wider uses. The great temples of the Classical era, such as the Parthenon in Athens, Greece, required giant statues of gods and goddesses and relief sculpture for friezes.

During the Hellenistic period, sculpture became more expressive and emotional. The 'Winged Victory of Samothrace' is a masterpiece of the sculptor's art. The draped garments in the sculpture appear to be rippling in a strong breeze.

A painting by Lawrence Alma-Tadema (left) depicts Phidias, the sculptor, painter and architect, showing the frieze of the Parthenon to his friends.

'Winged Victory of Samothrace', 2nd century BCE

Pottery and mosaics

Greek vase-painting, with painted figures, reached its peak from 600 to 350 BCE. There were two main styles, black-figure on red (700 BCE onwards) and red-figure on black (from about 530 BCE). The painted scenes give insights into the lives and beliefs of the ancient Greeks. Surviving floor mosaics (pictures and patterns made from small pieces of coloured glass, stone or other materials) also show scenes from life and mythology.

black-figure kylix by Exekias, 530 BCE

mosaic of a deer hunt, from a wealthy person's home at Pella, Macedonia, late 4th century BCE

THE ANCIENT WORLD
ROMAN ART

THE ART OF ANCIENT ROME WAS GENERALLY COPIED FROM THE WORKS OF ANCIENT GREEKS AND SOME FROM THE ETRUSCANS AND EGYPTIANS. SCULPTURE WAS CONSIDERED THE HIGHEST FORM OF ART, BUT FIGURE PAINTING WAS ALSO HIGHLY REGARDED. GREEK ARTISTS WERE ADMIRED, BUT MOST ROMAN ARTISTS WERE CONSIDERED TRADESMEN.

'Laocoön and His Sons' was highly praised by the Roman writer on art, Pliny the Elder. He thought it was the work of three Greek sculptors from the island of Rhodes.

Sculptures and paintings

Pliny recorded that most forms of art were more advanced in ancient Greek times than in Rome. Many Roman artists came from Greek colonies and provinces. Roman art was seen as decoration rather than appreciated for its own sake. It was specially ordered, owned in greater quantities and was adapted to more uses than Greek art. Wealthy Romans decorated their walls with art and their homes with sculptures and decorative objects.

Most wall painting was done using the secco (dry) method, but some fresco paintings also existed in Roman times. The main development compared with Greek art was the painting of landscapes where textures, shading and colour were shown realistically.

landscape mural at Pompeii

Antistius Labeon shows his paintings to clients (left). He was a Roman artist who lived during the reign of Vespasian and was also a government official. He was noted for painting the domestic life of ancient Rome.

Sculptural change

'Constantine's Arch', in Rome, is an important example of the stylistic changes of 4th century Roman art. The classical sculpture of the late Roman period began to disappear, a sign that the city was in decline. Sculptures of figures with realistic proportions are gone. Heads are too large, bodies are square and legs are stubby. Details and textures are missing as faces are roughly chiselled rather than modelled smoothly. Clothing folds are sculpted in very basic forms.

The 'Liberalitas' frieze on 'Constantine's Arch' shows Constantine giving money to the people.

MEDIEVAL ART
EUROPE, MIDDLE EAST AND NORTH AFRICA

WESTERN MEDIEVAL ART LASTED MORE THAN 1,000 YEARS. IT STARTED WITH EARLY CHRISTIAN AND BYZANTINE ART AND WAS FOLLOWED BY THE ART OF MANUSCRIPT ILLUMINATION DURING THE DARK AGES OF THE 5TH TO 10TH CENTURIES. LATER, MEDIEVAL ART WAS DOMINATED BY ROMANESQUE AND GOTHIC ART.

Virgin Enthroned with Two Saints, 6th century, St. Catherine's Monastery, Egypt

Early Christian to Romanesque art

Medieval art was produced in many ways such as painted religious icons, sculptures, illustrated manuscripts, stained glass, frescoes, textiles and mosaics.

The earliest surviving Christian art is found on the walls of Christian tombs in the catacombs of Rome from the late 2nd to early 4th centuries. In the East painted icons appeared showing images of Mary, Christ and the disciples. 'Virgin Enthroned with Two Saints' is one of the earliest that has been preserved.

The Prophet Daniel, late 11th century, stained glass from Augsburg Cathedral, Germany

Illuminated manuscripts, painted by monks, were the main form of painting that survived the period after the collapse of the Roman empire known as the Dark Ages. The 'Lindisfarne Gospels' is an example of Dark Ages painting.

Folio 27r from the Lindisfarne Gospels, 698, Eadfrith

Artists and sculptors during the Romanesque period (around the 10th to 13th centuries) produced religious scenes that decorated the walls and stained glass windows of churches.

Bayeux Tapestry (detail), 1066. English artists working in the traditional Anglo-Saxon style produced this memorial to the Battle of Hastings.

Maestà of Duccio, 1308–1311, by Duccio di Buoninsegna is a perfect example of religious Italian Gothic art of the early 14th century, in Siena, Italy. The figures are beautifully painted but lack the realism introduced by Giotto (1266–1337).

Resurrection of Christ, 1450–1490, English Nottingham alabaster panelled altarpiece (right)

Gothic art

Gothic art developed in France out of Romanesque art and spread to all of western Europe. It continued to grow and change until the late 15th century. In paintings, images of the Virgin Mary changed from the stiff, iconic look of Byzantium to pictures of a loving mother. Sculpture became more natural looking and three-dimensional as friezes stood out farther from their backgrounds.

THE REBIRTH OF CLASSICAL ART
THE RENAISSANCE

R ENAISSANCE ART – MEANING 'REBIRTH' – EMERGED AS A STYLE IN ITALY DURING THE 14TH CENTURY, ALONG WITH DEVELOPMENTS IN MUSIC, LITERATURE AND SCIENCE. A REVIVAL OF INTEREST IN THE CLASSICAL ART OF ANCIENT ROME, ALONG WITH THE RISE OF HUMANISM, HAD A BIG IMPACT ON ITS NATURAL AND REALISTIC LOOK.

The Betrayal of Christ, 1303–1306, Giotto di Bondone

The Tribute Money, 1426–1428, Masaccio

Giotto and realism

Giotto di Bondone is considered the first in a line of great artists who contributed to the beginning of Renaissance art. His intense and dramatic 'The Betrayal of Christ', (one of the Arena Chapel frescoes in Padua, Italy) is known for its natural poses and painting of the figures. The impact of the frescoes was recognised, even in Giotto's lifetime, as introducing a new style of realistic art.

At the beginning of the 15th century, another great artist appeared who painted scenes with lifelike figures and movements as well as a convincing sense of a three-dimensional view. In his short life, Tommaso di Ser Giovanni di Simone (known as Masaccio) had a big influence on artists who saw his work. He died when he was only 26 years old.

*A scene showing the artist, Piero della Francesca, painting **The Resurrection**, 1463–1465. Fresco paintings required the artist to paint on wet plaster, specially applied in sections onto a wall.*

Northern Renaissance

From the late 15th century, Italian Renaissance ideas spread across Europe. Trade and business in cities such as Bruges and Antwerp brought people together and increased the exchange of ideas between Italy, Belgium and the Netherlands. Northern Renaissance art, however, is seen as separate from Italian Renaissance humanism. Realism in the paintings of Jan and Hubert van Eyck and Robert Campin in the Netherlands and the fresh styles of Hieronymous Bosch and the German, Albrecht Durer, included scenes from everyday life as well as religious themes.

The Arnolfini Portrait, 1434, Jan van Eyck

Ghent Altarpiece (centre piece), 1426–1432, Hubert van Eyck and Jan van Eyck

Battle of San Romano, 1440–1450, Paolo Uccello

Perspective and mythology

Understanding of perspective is an important element in the paintings of the 15th century. Paolo Uccello's 'Battle of San Romano' (one in a series of three), is noted for its use of perspective. The broken lances lying on the ground create clear visual lines of perspective, known as linear perspective.

Piero della Francesca's deep interest in the study of perspective and his way of drawing people in natural poses is evident in all his work. His painting 'The Resurrection' contains a self-portrait of the artist as one of the sleeping soldiers.

Botticelli was the first Renaissance artist to paint mythological scenes on a large scale. His 'Primavera' shows Venus, the three Graces and Flora, who turns into spring and showers the world with flowers. Botticelli used symbols with meanings in his paintings and combined classical and Renaissance ideas of beauty and nature in many of his works.

Primavera, 1482, Sandro Botticelli

The Mérode Altarpiece, 1427–1432, *Master of Flémalle (Robert Campin)*

The Garden of Earthly Delights, 1500, by Hieronymous Bosch *is a warning about the perils of life's temptations. It shows God presenting Eve to Adam, a scene of figures and bizarre animals in a fantastical landscape, and a scene of hell.*

LIGHT, COLOUR AND STYLE
HIGH RENAISSANCE TO MANNERISM

THE HEIGHT OF THE ITALIAN RENAISSANCE ARRIVED AT THE BEGINNING OF THE 16TH CENTURY, BEST KNOWN FOR THE ART OF LEONARDO DA VINCI, MICHELANGELO AND RAPHAEL. CENTRED IN ROME IT WAS MATCHED ONLY IN VENICE BY THE COLOURFUL ART OF BELLINI AND TITIAN. HIGH RENAISSANCE WAS FOLLOWED BY MANNERISM AFTER THE SACK OF ROME IN 1527.

Mona Lisa, 1503–1506,
Leonardo da Vinci

High Renaissance in Rome

The High Renaissance produced some of the greatest painters of all time. Leonardo da Vinci was an Italian polymath and is regarded as the prime example of 'Renaissance Man'. Famous mainly as a painter, da Vinci crearted the 'Mona Lisa', probably the best known portrait in the world. His oil painting technique, called sfumato, uses blurring effects where distant objects appear hazy and bluer the farther away they are. This creates an atmospheric perspective instead of the linear perspective of earlier Renaissance art.

While da Vinci worked in Florence, two of the most important artists of the time were creating art

The School of Athens, 1510–1512, Raphael

in Rome where the High Renaissance flourished. Pope Julius II asked Raphael to decorate some rooms, known today as the four Raphael Rooms. The deep linear perspective of the 'The School of Athens' creates an impression of depth and is a masterpiece of drawing and design. It portrays many of history's greatest thinkers, together in one place and time to contribute to the common intelligence of humanity, echoing the heart of the Renaissance.

Italian Mannerism

Mannerism flourished in the 16th century between the Renaissance and Baroque styles. High Renaissance art emphasised balance of form and ideal beauty. Mannerism's exaggeration of these points resulted in images that are elegant but in unnatural ways. Elongated dimensions and unlikely poses with no clear perspective are typical. In Jacopo Pontormo's 'The Deposition of Christ', the awkward poses and unrealistic arrangement are a clear change from High Renaissance art. In Parmigianino's Mannerist painting, 'Madonna with the Long Neck', the extra-long dimensions of the figures, especially in the baby Jesus, are clear.

The Deposition of Christ
1525–1528, Pontormo

Madonna of the Long Neck
1534–1540, Parmigianino

Sistine Chapel Ceiling, 1508–1512, Michelangelo

Considered to be the greatest living artist during his lifetime, Michelangelo sculpted several masterpieces such as the 'Pietà' (the Virgin Mary cradling the dead body of Jesus). He also painted the most influential frescoes in the history of Western art, the 'Sistine Chapel Ceiling'. Michelangelo's highly personal style and twisting poses directly influenced Mannerism.

Pietà, 1498–1499, Michelangelo

Venetian Renaissance

Venice, with its colourful buildings and light that reflects from the lagoon it was built on, had a profound effect on its artists. One in particular, Giovanni Bellini, transformed Venice into a major centre of art that rivalled Rome and Florence. The colour, light and mood in Bellini's oil paintings showed he could achieve effects that were not possible with tempera. One of his students, Titian, went on to revolutionise all types of painting, from altarpieces to mythological works. Developing a free and expressive style in his oil paintings, he influenced later artists such as Velazquez in Spain and Flemish painter, Rubens.

The Doge Leonardo Loredan, 1501, Giovanni Bellini

Bacchus and Ariadne, 1520–1523, by Titian, whose bright colours and expressive poses of figures against a luscious landscape create a vivid scene. It is typical of the Venetian Renaissance.

Mannerism outside Italy

Mannerism arrived in France at the Court of Francis I. The school of Fontainbleau was founded there in the 1530s by the Italian artists, Rosso Fiorentino and Primaticcio. The style later spread through Europe. By the end of the century, the unusual Mannerist art of El Greco was adorning the walls of churches in Toledo, Spain. In his 'The Burial of the Count of Orgaz', the Mannerist method of design is clearly expressed with stretched forms and a lack of horizon. In northern Europe the Flemish created a different style of Mannerism. In England, Nicholas Hilliard painted stylish miniatures that follow the Mannerist influence of the Fontainbleau school.

Young Man Among Roses, 1547, Nicholas Hilliard

The Burial of the Count of Orgaz, 1586, El Greco

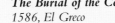

DYNAMIC GRANDEUR TO DELICATE ELEGANCE
BAROQUE AND ROCOCO

In response to the Protestant Reformation, the Catholic Church stated that the arts should communicate religious themes with direct and emotional involvement. As a result the Baroque style of the 1600s began to flourish. By the late 1720s, Rococo took over from it as a reaction against Baroque's grandeur and strict regulations.

***The Martyrdom of St. Peter**, 1601, Caravaggio*

***Domine, Quo Vadis?**, 1601, Annibale Carracci*

Italian Baroque

The Baroque style began in Rome where Caravaggio and Annibale Carracci created many masterpieces. They both painted in oils but had different styles. Carravagio painted scenes with realistic figures and dramatic light. Carracci's paintings have figures in the exaggerated poses and bright colours influenced by the Venetian School. Baroque soon spread to other cities and countries.

Baroque outside Italy

The Baroque style of art flourished throughout Europe. The influential artist Peter Paul Rubens introduced it into the Catholic countries of the Spanish Netherlands and Spain. Paintings by Spanish artist Velazquez show masterful brushwork, while Rembrandt and Vermeer in the Netherlands have strength and energy in their portraits. The start of the 17th century in France saw a change to a more exciting Baroque style. Caravaggio-inspired paintings by Georges de La Tours and colourful works by Poussin are examples of this.

***The Fall of Phaeton**, 1604, Peter Paul Rubens*

***The Night Watch**, 1642, Rembrandt*

One of the greatest decorative painters of 18th-century Europe, Giovanni Battista Tiepolo painted frescoes in Italy, Germany and Spain. His works in the New Residenz palace in Würzburg, Germany, included a ceiling fresco – at 677 square metres (7,287 square feet), the largest in the world. Some paintings contain trompe l'oeil where figures appear to come out over the edge of the frame.

Fresco in the Würzburg Residence, 1751, *Giovanni Battista Tiepolo*

Rococo

Rococo developed in the early 18th century in Paris, France. Artists used a more decorative and elegant spirit in their work. François Boucher was the most well-known painter of the Rococo, but Jean-Honoré Fragonard produced one of its most famous works in 'The Swing'.

The Swing, 1767, Jean-Honoré Fragonard

The pink frilly dress of the swinging girl is caught by sunlight shining through an opening in a beautiful wooded garden. Rococo soon spread throughout Europe where it developed distinct styles in different countries. In England, Thomas Gainsborough painted portraits combined with landscapes, producing a more conservative style of Rococo.

Mr and Mrs Andrews, 1750, *Thomas Gainsborough*

Girl with a Pearl Earring, 1665, *Johannes Vermeer*

The Surrender of Breda, 1634–1635, by Diego Velazquez perfectly captures the respect in which Spinola is held – one of the most humane generals of his time.

The Dance to the Music of Time, 1640, by Nicolas Poussin who was the leading painter of the classical French Baroque style, although he spent most of his working life in Rome.

Joseph the Carpenter, 1642, Georges de La Tours

REDISCOVERY AND REACTION
NEOCLASSICISM AND ROMANTICISM

DURING THE LATE 18TH AND EARLY 19TH CENTURIES, ARTISTS WERE INSPIRED BY THE CULTURE OF ANCIENT ROME. ARTISTS OF THIS NEOCLASSICISM (NEW CLASSICAL MOVEMENT) CARED MORE ABOUT HISTORICAL ACCURACY. THIS PERIOD WAS FOLLOWED BY ROMANTICISM, WHICH REACTED AGAINST THE ORDER OF NEOCLASSICISM.

The Oath of the Horatii, 1784, Jacques-Louis David

Canova's sculpture 'Psyche Revived by Cupid's Kiss' is regarded as a masterpiece of Neoclassical sculpture. It portrays the mythological lovers with great tenderness, characteristic of the later movement of Romanticism.

Psyche Revived by Cupid's Kiss, 1787, is by Antonio Canova. Canova was painted in his studio with a plaster model of Psyche and Cupid without his wings.

Napoleon I on his Imperial Throne, 1806, Jean-Auguste-Dominique Ingres

Neoclassicism

The discoveries at Pompeii and Herculaneum in the 1700s encouraged fresh interest in the ancient world and inspired artists to produce Neoclassical paintings. The success of David's 'Oath of the Horatii' at the Paris Salon of 1785 showed a Classical style in which the heroic figures are posed in side-view as if in a sculpted frieze.

Another French Neoclassic artist, Ingres was inspired by the ancient Greek giant 'Statue of Zeus' at Olympia in Greece when he painted a portrait of French emperor Napoleon Bonaparte in his robes.

The Romantic landscape

At the start of the 19th century, artists began to look at nature with fresh eyes. It could be painted in all its majesty and, as important, could also inspire thoughts and feelings. In some artists, such as Samuel Palmer and Caspar David

A Dream in the Apennines, 1864, Samuel Palmer

Friedrich, the landscape revealed God's hand. Others, such as John Constable and Thomas Cole, were in awe of the beauty of nature. The power and force of nature is most brilliantly captured by Turner's land and seascapes. His mastery of light, as in 'The Fighting Temeraire', shows the end of an era as a steam tug tows a sailship to its end at sunset.

The Hay Wain, 1821, John Constable

Romanticism

Romantic artists were influenced by the difficulties of revolution and the ideas of freedom that inspired the music and writing of the time. The art included a variety of styles. William Blake, who produced highly finished illustrations to accompany texts, was one of the key figures of Romanticism. In Henry Fuseli, in England, it inspired the theatrical, with 'The Nightmare' showing a sleeping woman being visited by a mare, a mythological evil spirit. In France artists such as Géricault and Delacroix produced paintings of a heroic nature. Géricault's 'The Charging Chasseur' has a dramatic composition and is painted with strong, energetic brushstrokes.

The Nightmare, 1781,
Henry Fuseli

The Third of May 1808, *1814,*
Francisco de Goya

In Germany religiously inspired subjects were painted by artists such as Philipp Otto Runge. In Spain the horrors of the Peninsular War inspired Goya to paint his masterpiece, 'The Third of May 1808'. Drama and horror combine in a scene of death and defiance. The central figure with his arms outstretched, recalling Christ on the cross, faces execution by a French firing squad.

The Charging
Chasseur,
1812,
Théodore
Géricault

The Pre-Raphaelite Brotherhood

Founded in 1848 the Pre-Raphaelite Brotherhood artists were John Everett Millais, Dante Gabriel Rossetti and William Holman Hunt. Their inspiration was from Italian painting before the time of Raphael. They painted brightly coloured scenes from the Bible, mythology and literature in careful detail. Millais's 'Ophelia' pictures the drowning heroine from Shakespeare's Hamlet in great detail.

Ophelia, *1851,*
John Everett Millais

The Fighting Temeraire, tugged to her last berth to be broken up, 1839, J. M. W. Turner

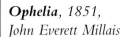

The Oxbow, 1836, Thomas Cole

Wanderer above the
Sea of Fog, *1818,*
Caspar David Friedrich

REAL LIFE
REALISM, IMPRESSIONISM AND POST-IMPRESSIONISM

In the middle of the 19th century, artists started looking at the realities of life. Rural workers were no longer shown in idealised settings but in hard-working everyday roles. The artists' wish to break free from traditional painting encouraged them to paint ordinary scenes outdoors rather than in the studio.

The Stonebreakers, 1849, Gustave Courbet

REALISM

Realism began in France in the late 1840s, led by Gustave Courbet. He believed that art should concentrate on reality, the way things really were. His paintings of labourers and peasants in the countryside, such as 'The Stonebreakers' (1849), showed the hardship of country life. His use of the palette knife in some of his works, loading paint heavily onto the canvas, differed from the carefully finished traditional art of the academy. French artists Jean-Francois Millet and Honoré Daumier and Englishman Henry Wallis were also Realists.

During the late 1870s, a group of Russian artists known as the Wanderers also took up Realism. Across the Atlantic in the United States, artists such as Thomas Eakins were producing Realism masterpieces such as his 'The Gross Clinic'.

IMPRESSIONISM

In the late 1860s, a group of artists around Paris shared a desire to break free from the constraints of the highly finished art of the academy. They portrayed scenes of everyday life with brushstrokes that captured the impression of light and colour in a fleeting moment.

The Gross Clinic, 1875, Thomas Eakins (right)

The Gleaners, 1857, Jean-François Millet

Barge Haulers on the Volga, 1873, Ilya Repin

The Gallery

Millet's 'The Gleaners' is famous for featuring peasants in a sympathetic way. Eakins's 'The Gross Clinic' is known for its bloody and very blunt painting of surgery. Ilya Repin was a member of the Wanderers. His painting of men hauling a barge shows the real hardship of life in Russia. The young man looking up as if to break free, and a steamship in the distance, tell of a changing future.

Haystacks (sunset), 1890–1891, by Claude Monet is one of several paintings of haystacks in the field. Monet shows differences in quality of light at various times of day, seasons and weather.

The main artists involved, called Impressionists, were Frédéric Bazille, Paul Cézanne, Edgar Degas, Edouard Manet, Claude Monet, Berthe Morisot, Camille Pissarro, Pierre-August Renoir and Alfred Sisley. They rejected the official exhibitions shown in the Paris Salon and exhibited in smaller places in Paris. Their style and ideas spread beyond France to the rest of Europe and the United States.

The Impressionists left their studios and travelled into the countryside and towns to paint outdoors. **Claude Monet Painting by the Edge of a Wood,** *1888, is by John Singer Sargent (detail).*

POST-IMPRESSIONISM

Developed roughly between 1886 and 1905, the Post-Impressionist art movement embraced Impressionist values. It continued to use bright, strong colours and real-life subject matter. But its artists were not satisfied with simply recording the scene in front of them.

Artists such as Georges Seurat created images from tiny dots of paint, a technique called pointilism. Paul Cézanne experimented with angular forms. Another important artist was Paul Gauguin. He is recognised for his use of very bright colour and inclusion of Tahitian subjects. The most famous of the Post-Impressionists is Vincent van Gogh, whose use of vivid colours with descriptive brushstrokes strongly conveyed emotions and feelings.

Self Portrait, *1889, by Vincent van Gogh is one of the artist's many self portraits, more than 43 between 1885 and 1889. They are painted with intense self-scrutiny and use colours and brushstrokes that aim to reflect his emotions at the time of painting.*

Dance at le Moulin de la Galette, 1876, Pierre-Auguste Renoir (left)

Mont Sainte-Victoire, about 1887, Paul Cézanne (right)

The Midday Nap, 1894, Paul Gauguin

Renoir painted 'Dance at le Moulin de la Galette' outdoors using models and friends to pose. The wind nearly blew the canvas away.

Cézanne used geometry to describe nature and different colours to represent the depth of objects. He is said to be the 'Father of Cubism'.

Gauguin's art is described as 'Primitivism', which was inspired by art from non-Western or prehistoric peoples.

IMAGINATION AND EMOTIONS
SYMBOLISM AND EXPRESSIONISM

Towards the end of the 19th century, writers and artists in Europe decided to break with the past and began producing works of imagination and emotion. Strong feelings were shown in some artists' work through ideas and symbols. Others used strong colours and distorted images.

The Apparition, *1876, Gustave Moreau*

Symbolism

The beginnings of Symbolism can be traced back to the paintings of French artists Gustave Moreau and Pierre Puvis de Chavannes in the 1860s and 1870s. Both artists painted romantic subjects but concentrated on emotions. What they and other Symbolist artists had in common was a mood rather than a style. In 'The Apparition' Moreau portrays the head of John the Baptist

I Lock My Door Upon Myself, *1891, Fernand Khnopff*

The Kiss, *1907, Gustav Klimt*

floating in front of the princess Salome. The painting's scary subject and pretty female figure are just two of the Symbolist artists' most common themes. Fernand Khnopff's 'I Lock My Door Upon Myself' shows a mysterious and haunting scene cluttered with items that hint at hidden meanings. These symbolic details suggest the inward-looking and spiritual interests of the Symbolist artist.

Mental intensity, sex and death were also ingredients of the Symbolists' art, as seen in the works of Gustav Klimt and others of the Vienna Secession (a group of Austrian artists). Klimt's 'The Kiss', painted in his gilded style (where gold leaf was applied), shows a couple in robes decorated in a style influenced by the Art Nouveau movement.

Art Nouveau

Art Nouveau was an art style embracing architecture, graphic art, interior design and the decorative arts, as well as the fine arts. Its name comes from The Maison de l'Art Nouveau (House of New Art), which was the name of the gallery opened in Paris in 1895 that featured exclusively modern art. Art Nouveau has close connections with the Pre-Raphaelites and the Symbolist styles, which include artists such as Aubrey Beardsley, Alphonse Mucha, Edward Burne-Jones, Gustav Klimt and Jan Toorop. The posters for the Moulin Rouge theatre by the Post-Impressionist Henri de Toulouse-Lautrec are also part of this style.

Divan Japonais, *1892–93, lithograph by Henri de Toulouse-Lautrec*

The Arts, Dance, *1898, Alphonse Mucha*

The Scream, 1893, Edvard Munch

Expressionism

Beginning in Germany at the start of the 20th century, artists of this modernist movement produced art for emotional effect in order to inspire moods or ideas. Several years before Expressionism was recognised, Norwegian artist Edvard Munch painted 'The Scream'. Vibrant with distorted shapes, it influenced many later Expressionist artists.

Up until 1914 Russian artist Kandinsky spent many holidays in Murnau in the Bavarian Alps, where he painted scenes in a colourful Expressionist manner. His geometric forms are a sign of his later abstract style.

Street in Murnau, A Village Street, 1908, Wassily Kandinsky

Blue Horse I, 1911, Franz Marc

Franz Marc, a painter and printmaker, was one of the key figures of the German Expressionist movement. Most of his work portrays animals painted in bright primary colours and in an almost Cubist manner, simply and with emotion.

German Ernst Ludwig Kirchner was one of the founders of the artists' group Die Brücke (The Bridge), a group that led to the foundation of Expressionism. Along with his fellow artists, he wanted to break away from the academic style and find a new style of artistic expression. His street scenes expressed the loneliness he felt in a large and unfriendly city.

Berlin Street Scene, 1913, Ernst Ludwig Kirchner

Henri Matisse

A brilliant painter, theatre designer and illustrator, Henri Matisse became one of the most important artists of the 20th century. His pure and intense use of colour defined his work. Along with André Derain, he founded the Fauvism movement (1904–1908). Les Fauves is French for 'The Wild Beasts', after an art critic's criticism of the artists' exhibition. Matisse's works, however, emphasised strong colour and simple shapes, which had a great influence on the Expressionists.

illustration of Henri Matisse painting

MODERNISM
CUBISM AND ABSTRACT ART

ONE OF THE THE MOST INFLUENTIAL ART MOVEMENTS OF THE 20TH CENTURY, CUBISM EVOLVED DURING THE DEVELOPMENT OF CARS, PLANES AND PHOTOGRAPHY. ORIGINALLY INSPIRED BY THE WORKS OF THE POST-IMPRESSIONIST PAUL CEZANNE, ITS MOST FAMOUS ARTISTS WERE PABLO PICASSO AND GEORGES BRAQUE.

The Knifegrinder, 1912–1913, Kazimir Malevich

Woman in Blue, 1912, Fernand Léger

of Futurism as well as the geometric shapes related to Cubism. The early work of Fernand Léger shows cubed forms painted in patches with primary colours – typical of Cubist art.

Cubism

In Cubist art, scenes are often painted from various viewpoints, broken up and reassembled in abstracted and box-like forms that still contain some visual references to the original scenes. Cubism had a far-reaching and wide-ranging effect, and variations appeared in several countries from Vorticism in England to Futurism in Italy. 'The Knifegrinder' by Russian artist Kazimir Malevich is regarded as a Cubo-Futurist painting. It contains the abstraction

Braque and Picasso often met to discuss their work. Some of their Cubist paintings were so close in style, critics found it difficult to know whose they were.

Vorticism

Started in 1913, a year before the outbreak of World War I (1914–1918), Vorticism was a short-lived movement in Britain. The style came from Cubism but was closer to Italian Futurism, influenced by the power of the machine age. Strong lines and bold colours are typical of the movement. Vorticism broke up in 1915 due to the war.

Dazzle-ships in Drydock at Liverpool, 1919, Edward Wadsworth

Composition VI, *1913, Wassily Kandinsky*

Abstract art

The most lasting art form of the 20th century is Abstract art, which in its most extreme form shows no relation to recognisable subjects. It is sometimes called 'non-objective art'. The first examples appeared soon after 1910. Russian artist Wassily Kandinsky was inspired by the composer Arnold Schoenberg's avant garde work. He produced a series of abstract paintings known as Compositions. Three were destroyed in World War II (1939–1945). His 'Composition VI' evokes a flood, baptism, destruction and rebirth on a large wood panel.

Founded by Kazimir Malevich in Russia, Suprematism was an art movement that used geometric forms, such as circles, squares, lines and rectangles, painted in a simple range of colours. His 'Suprematist Composition' represents a collection of

Suprematist Composition, *1916, Kazimir Malevich*

geometric forms and colour on a harsh white background.

De Stijl (The Style) was a Dutch artistic movement founded in 1917 in Amsterdam that favoured pure abstraction. Piet Mondrian was the most famous of its artists. His 'Composition II in Red, Blue and Yellow' is typical of the movement with its simplified composition of vertical and

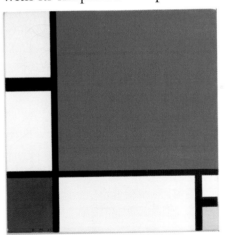

horizontal black lines and bold primary colours on white backgrounds.

Composition II in Red, Blue and Yellow, *1930, Piet Mondrian*

Futurism

Cubism contributed to the formation of Italy's Futurism style, and in its turn Futurism influenced the art movements of Art Deco, Constructivism, Surrealism and Dada. Originating in Italy in the early 20th century, Futurism emphasised speed and the technology of the day – such as the car, train and the aeroplane. Italian artist Umberto Boccioni, one of the foremost Futurists, clearly showed Futurism's love of speed and included the expression of movement in his paintings and sculpture.

Dynamism of a Cyclist, *1913 (above) and* **Unique Forms of Continuity in Space**, *1913 (right), Umberto Boccioni*

23

ABSURDITY AND THE UNCONSCIOUS MIND
DADA, SURREALISM AND ABSTRACT EXPRESSIONISM

DADA WAS AN ART MOVEMENT THAT APPEARED AS A DIRECT REACTION TO THE SLAUGHTER OF WORLD WAR I. DADA WAS SHORT-LIVED AND WAS REPLACED BY SURREALISM – A MOVEMENT THAT CONCENTRATED ON THE DREAMWORLD AND THE UNCONSCIOUSNESS OF THE MIND. THIS IN TURN INFLUENCED ABSTRACT EXPRESSIONISM IN NEW YORK IN THE 1940S.

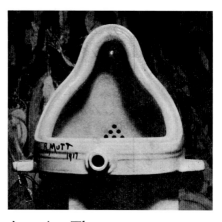

Fountain, 1917,
Marcel Duchamp

Dada

The Dada art movement had artists in Europe and North America. They were not connected by an artistic style but by a reaction against patriotism and the brutality of war that it created. They chose not to follow any form of art. To some Dada artists such as George Grosz, their art was anti-art and was created to shock. Frenchman Marcel Duchamp was an important conceptual artist during the first half of the 20th century. His works such as 'Fountain', a 'readymade' (not made by the artist) piece of sculpture, uses an ordinary object as a piece of Dada anti-art. Entered into an exhibition in New York in 1917, it was rejected even though the rules stated that all works would be accepted.

Surrealism

André Breton, a French poet, founded Surrealism. He described it in his 'Manifesto of Surrealism' as able to express what and how the mind thought. Surrealist artists took up this theme using various techniques to paint and sculpt thoughts and the unconscious, such as dreams, either in abstract form or with realistic precision.

The Persistence of Memory,
1931, Salvador Dali

Dali worked with many photographers. **Dali Atomicus**, *1948, was photographed by Philippe Halsman.*

Joan Miró

A Spanish painter and sculptor, Joan Miró had contempt for conventional methods of painting and continually experimented with his style of art. He is best known for those of his paintings that portray many abstract shapes alongside recognisable forms in a three-dimensional space. Although he did not identify consistently with a particular style of art he is regarded as a Surrealist. In his 'Harlequin's Carnival' Miró paints the harlequin as a strange, guitar-like figure with a long neck and a round, mustachioed head. All around him bizarre creatures and shapes dance in a dream-like manner.

Harlequin's Carnival, 1924–1925, Joan Miró

Pietà or Revolution by Night, 1923, Max Ernst

The Son of Man, 1946, René Magritte

Some of the most well-known artists of the Surrealist movement had varying styles. Max Ernst used mixed styles of flat colour and shaded forms in his 'Pietà or Revolution by Night', which replaces the Virgin Mary holding the body of Christ with an image of the artist held by his father.

One of the best known Surrealists was Spanish artist Salvador Dali. One of his most famous works, 'The Persistence of Memory' features melting watches in a dream-like landscape painted in a highly detailed way. The painting echoes German scientist Albert Einstein's theories of time and relativity, the major scientific idea of the century.

Questioning the state of reality was an important trait of Surrealist artist René Magritte. His witty and thought-provoking art showed unusual positioning of objects that give an unreal and dream-like quality to his images.

Abstract Expressionism

Many artists fleeing World War II in Europe arrived in New York. Among them were many Surrealist painters such as Salvador Dali and Max Ernst. After the war a new movement appeared that put New York at the centre of the art world, rivalling Paris. Artists such as Willem de Kooning, Jackson Pollock and Mark Rothko used individual and different styles to show emotion in abstract form. Pollock's original paintings were created by dripping and swishing paint across large canvases laid out on the floor.

Rothko painted in oil and only on large canvases designed to overwhelm the viewer. He even recommended that viewers stand as little as 45 centimetres (18 inches) away from the canvas.

No. 61 (Rust and Blue), 1953, Mark Rothko

Self Portrait with Necklace of Thorns, 1940, Frida Kahlo

Frida Kahlo

Mexican painter Frida Kahlo lived and painted in Mexico City in the first half of the 20th century. She is most famous for her self portraits. Her dream-like paintings have sometimes given her a Surrealist label, but she rejected it. She was often isolated while recovering from health problems caused by a traffic accident when she was a teenager.

POPULAR CULTURE AND OPTICAL ILLUSION
POP AND OP ART

POP ART WAS BORN IN THE 1950S IN POST-WAR BRITAIN AND GAINED RECOGNITION AT THE MAJOR ART EXHIBIT 'THIS IS TOMORROW'. IT BECAME PART OF A TREND IN CULTURE WHERE THE YOUNGER GENERATION WAS MAKING ITS VOICE HEARD IN FASHION AND MUSIC. DURING THE 1960S DAZZLING, ABSTRACT ART ALSO CAME INTO FASHION.

I was a Rich Man's Plaything, 1947, *Eduardo Paolozzi*

Pop art

The formation of the British art collective in 1952, known as the Independent Group, is seen as the beginning of Pop art. One of its founders, Eduardo Paolozzi produced collages (various pictures glued together on a backing) from images taken from American advertisements and comics. His 'I was a Rich Man's Plaything' is typical of his work and is one of Pop art's earliest examples.

American artists soon took notice. They began to produce works using pictures of film stars and advertising images that appeared in the booming U.S. society of the 1950s, following the difficult ecomonic conditions after World War II. Andy Warhol is probably the best known artist of the Pop art movement in the United States. He used images of American advertising campaigns such as Campbell's soup cans and Hollywood film stars such as Marilyn Monroe. He gradually stopped painting in favour of screen printing. He employed a studio of people he called the 'Factory' in New York City.

Jasper Johns

Not all art critics consider Jasper Johns to be a Pop artist. He is often regarded as a Neo-Dadaist, which was happening at the same time as the Pop art movement. Much of his art, however, had many similarities to other Pop artists working at the same time. His paintings often include images and objects from popular culture. He used media such as encaustic (heated beeswax with coloured pigments added), which he painted over a collage made from found materials such as newspaper. His 'Three Flags' shifts the emphasis from a respected national emblem, turning it into an object.

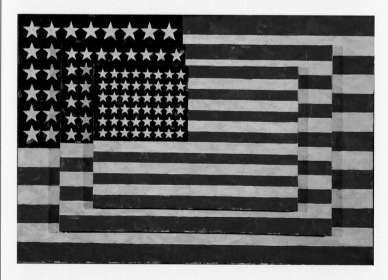

Three Flags, 1958, *Jasper Johns*

Warhol's prints display a relaxed approach in which mistakes and unintended marks become parts of the final images. The 'Marilyn Diptych' is regarded as one of his best works. It was completed just after Marilyn Monroe's death. The brightly coloured images on the left are repeated in black and white on the right. They convey the contrasting life of the star on screen and her troubled personal life and death.

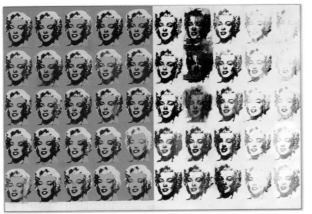

Marilyn Diptych, 1962, *Andy Warhol*

Another well known piece of art of the Pop scene is Roy Lichtenstein's 'Whaam!'. He painted many large images showing highly emotional content in what seems, at first glance, to be a graphic style. The obvious comic book imagery is used to illustrate the lack of thought and feeling in modern American culture.

British artist David Hockney spent a large part of his life in Los Angeles. His 'A Bigger Splash' showcases his Pop art theme. It shows Californian culture with its glamorous Hollywood connections and enviable outdoor lifestyle – around a large pool beneath blue skies.

Whaam!, 1963, *Roy Lichtenstein (below)*

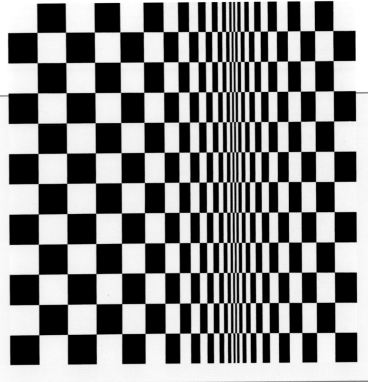

A Bigger Splash, 1967, *David Hockney (right)*

Op art

The term Op art was first used in 1964 to describe a form of abstract art that aims to trick the eye. It developed from Kinetic art, which first appeared in 1913 with Duchamp's 'Bicycle Wheel' and then took the form of sculpture in the 1950s and 1960s. Op art gives the illusion of movement on a two-dimensional surface. Bridget Riley, one of the most well-known Op artists, began with black and white artworks. Her 'Movement in Squares' is an example of how the eye is deceived by the geometric pattern of black and white squares. In later works Riley used lines of colour to create a shimmering illusion.

Movement in Squares, 1961, Bridget Riley

ART OF TODAY
POSTMODERN AND CONTEMPORARY ART

THE LATER HALF OF THE 20TH CENTURY SAW A REACTION TO MODERNISM WITH A MOVEMENT CALLED POSTMODERNISM. THIS HAD VARIOUS FORMS, INCLUDING PERFORMANCE ART, INSTALLATION ART, CONCEPTUAL ART AND MULTIMEDIA. CONTEMPORARY ART FOLLOWED ON FROM IT AS THE ART OF TODAY, INCLUDING MANY TYPES OF ART.

Fifty Days at Iliam: The Fire that Consumes All Before It, 1978, Cy Twombly

Pictures and words

Since the 1960s some artists have included words in their art to explore the nature of 'meaning'. American artist Cy Twombly brought an original approach to painting. Inspired by ancient mythology, he painted several pieces based on Homer's epic poem 'The Iliad', using words and images.

Exploring emptiness

Artists in the 1990s began exploring the concepts of time and space. One of the strangest is negative, or empty, space. British artist Rachel Whiteread created a concrete sculpture from the inside of a London house that was due to be demolished. This short-lived piece (it was knocked down a year later) captures the space in which we live, in the form of a spatial monument.

House, 1993, Rachel Whiteread

Natural Art

Some art is created to exist in a certain place. Known as site-specific art, the work of art is created at the site and cannot be moved. Many artists work in the natural landscape. 'Spiral Jetty', an earthwork sculpture created by American Robert Smithson, forms a 460-metre (1,500-foot) coil jutting from the shore of a lake. Scottish artist Andy Goldsworthy's work often includes flowers, icicles, leaves, mud, snow, stone, sticks, thorns and living trees to create sculptures that have a connection with the natural world.

Spiral Jetty, 1970, Robert Smithson

Graffiti art

Rooted in the artistic vandalism of New York in the 1980s, Graffiti art made a lasting mark on the world of art. Its key figures were Americans Jean-Michel Basquiat and Keith Haring. Although both artists painted on walls, Basquiat claimed to have nothing to do with Graffiti. Haring's work was often used to send a message. He reused the three monkeys (see, hear, speak no evil) for an AIDS awareness poster.

The Physical Impossibility of Death in the Mind of Someone Living, 1991, Damien Hirst

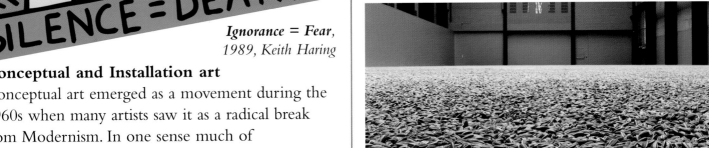

Ignorance = Fear, 1989, Keith Haring

Artists', created a Conceptual work of a shark in a tank of formaldehyde. Getting close to the work, the viewer is confronted with one of nature's killers but cannot imagine death.

Installation art was not regarded as a category of art until the mid-20th century. Installations are designed to change the way a space is viewed. Chinese artist Ai Weiwei's work covers the ground floor of the Tate museum in London with millions of painted porcelain (ceramic) seeds.

Conceptual and Installation art

Conceptual art emerged as a movement during the 1960s when many artists saw it as a radical break from Modernism. In one sense much of contemporary art can be viewed as Conceptual art. Damien Hirst, a member of the 'Young British

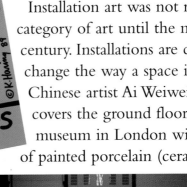

100 Million Porcelain Sunflowers, 2010, Ai Weiwei

American Gothic, 1930, Grant Wood

Figurative art

Throughout the 20th century, artists have continued to paint and sculpt in a figurative (realistic) way. Figurativism is often defined as the opposite of abstract art. It clearly represents the subject. Grant Wood's 'American Gothic' is one of the most famous paintings in American art. Painted in 1930 it became a symbol of the 1930s' Great Depression. Artists were disappointed with Conceptual art by the end of the 20th century. The 'Stuckism' art movement was founded in Britain in 1999 by Charles Thomson and Billy Childish. It promoted Figurative painting and the revival of experimenting with materials and techniques to create art that reflected modern society.

Clamming on Maud, 2013, Billy Childish

GLOSSARY

abstract art
Art that does not try to represent reality but uses colours, shapes, forms and textures to achieve a desired effect.

academic art
Art that is influenced by the standards of a national school that teaches art, known as an academy, such as the French Académie des Beaux-Arts.

AIDS
Acquired Immune Deficiency Syndrome caused by infection with the Human Immunodeficiency Virus (HIV) spread primarily by unprotected sex.

Art Deco
A decorative art style of the 1920s and 1930s, characterised by geometric shapes and clear and precise lines – seen mainly in household objects, transportation and in architecture.

avant garde
New and unusual or experimental ideas, especially in the arts.

Byzantium
The Byzantine Empire (also referred to as the Eastern Roman Empire), which was the continuation of the Roman Empire in the East with its capital city, Constantinople. It fell to the Ottoman Turks in 1453.

catacomb
An underground cemetery consisting of a gallery with recesses for tombs, such as those constructed by the ancient Romans.

Conceptual art
Art in which the artist's idea is considered more important than the finished product.

Constructivism
A movement in which assorted mechanical objects are combined into abstract, mobile, structural forms.

Etruscans
A little known civilisation of ancient Italy that existed from 700 BCE until it was absorbed into the Roman Republic with the Roman–Etruscan Wars in the late 4th century BCE.

Fayum mummy portraits
The modern term for a type of realistically-painted portrait of a person on wooden board – attached to mummies from the 3rd to the 9th centuries – found across Egypt and more commonly in the Fayum Basin in northern Egypt.

Figurative art
Art that is clearly representative of the objects the artist has chosen, in contrast to abstract art, but does not necessarily contain images of people.

formaldehyde
A fluid with many uses, including preserving organic tissue by delaying the speed of its decay.

fresco
A painting done rapidly in watercolour onto wet plaster on a wall or ceiling. The colours soak into the plaster and become fixed as they dry.

frieze
A short, wide section of a wall of a building usually with a painted decoration or a scene carved into it.

Humanism (Renaissance Humanism)
A Renaissance cultural movement that turned away from medieval teachings and revived ancient Greek and Roman thought.

Kinetic art
Art that seems to move as the viewer looks at it or depends on actual motion for its effect.

kylix
An ancient Greek cup with a shallow bowl and a tall stem used for wine.

megalith
A large stone, or a number of large stones, that forms a prehistoric monument.

Modernism
A movement in the arts that aimed to break with classical and traditional forms in the late 19th and early 20th centuries.

mythology
A collection of stories from ancient cultures that explain nature, history and creation as they knew it, which include heroes, monsters and gods.

Paleolithic
A prehistoric period of human history lasting from 2.6 million years ago to around 10,000 years ago, when early stone tools were developed.

Parthenon
The temple of the goddess Athena, built on the Acropolis in Greece in 447–432 BCE by Pericles to celebrate the Greek victory over the Persians.

perspective
The art of drawing objects on a two-dimensional surface, giving the correct impression of their height, width, depth and position in relation to each other when viewed from a single point.

pharaoh
The title for a king or queen of ancient Egypt.

polymath
A person of wide-ranging knowledge or learning in a number of subject areas.

Post-Modernism
A late-20th century style and concept in the arts, which was a reaction against Modernism. Typical features include a deliberate mixing of artistic styles and media, the use of earlier styles and images relating to people's obsession with buying things.

Primitivism
An art movement that took visuals from non-Western or prehistoric peoples. It also applies to those working in the style of naïve or folk art.

Protestant Reformation
A division of the Roman Catholic Church, started by Martin Luther in Germany, which resulted in most of northern Europe coming under the influence of Protestantism.

relief sculpture
A sculptural technique where the carved elements stand out but remain attached to the background.

screen printing
A printing method that forces ink through a fine screen onto a flat object such as paper or fabric to create an image.

secco method
A wall painting technique where colour paints are applied onto a dry plaster.

status
A person's accepted or official position.

tempera
Also known as egg tempera, it is a permanent, fast-drying painting method using coloured powder mixed with a binding agent such as egg yolk.

trompe l'oeil
An art technique that uses realistic images to create an optical illusion that makes images appear three dimensionally on a two-dimensional surface.

INDEX